JAWS
OF THE JERSEY SHORE

Patricia Heyer

Published by Arcadia Children's Books
A Division of Arcadia Publishing, Inc.
Charleston, SC
www.arcadiapublishing.com

Manufactured in the United States

Designed by Jessica Nevins
Images used courtesy of Shutterstock.com; p. 26 *The Philadelphia Inquirer*/
Philadelphia, Pennsylvania/Sat, Jul 15, 1916

ISBN 978-1-4671-9771-7
Library of Congress Control Number 2024934284

JAWS

OF THE JERSEY SHORE

by Patricia Heyer

Adapted from
Shark Attacks of the Jersey Shore
by Patricia & Robert Heyer

NEW YORK

SANDY HOOK BAY 6

MATAWAN CREEK 3

SANDY HOOK BEACH 1

SEA BRIGHT 6

LONG BRANCH 4

SPRING LAKE 3 & 8

PENNSYLVANIA

ADVENTURE AQUARIUM 8

SEASIDE PARK 2

BARNEGAT BAY 6

SURF CITY 2

BEACH HAVEN 3

NEW JERSEY

BRIGANTINE BEACH 1

ATLANTIC CITY 2 & 3

LONGPORT HARBOR 8

OCEAN CITY 1

GREAT EGG HARBOR INLET

2 & 5

SEA ISLE CITY 7

DELAWARE BAY 1

WILDWOOD 4

ATLANTIC OCEAN

ELAWARE

TABLE OF CONTENTS & MAP KEY

INTRODUCTION

What goes through your mind when you hear the word "shark"? Do you imagine dark, sinister eyes waiting for the right moment to ambush their prey? Does your blood run cold at the thought of a huge fin in the water . . . swimming straight for you? Gulp.

If you are like most people, you're probably as

fascinated as you are terrified of these fierce apex predators. After all, sharks have ruled the oceans for more than four hundred million years—even before dinosaurs roamed the earth. It's no wonder people line up like crazy for the latest blockbuster movie starring a killer shark, or watch *Shark Week* on TV year after year. We shiver at the sight of their sharp teeth and powerful jaws. We marvel at their stealth and speed. And sometimes, when we splash in the ocean waves, we find ourselves wondering . . . could there be a shark nearby?

The answer to this question might make chills run up and down your spine.

Sharks live in the ocean. They are *always* nearby.

So, chances are, if you've ever gone swimming at the beach, you've probably been a lot closer to a shark than you realize. The same thing is true right here at the Jersey Shore. Although most local sharks are harmless, run-ins can happen. In fact, since 1842, people and sharks down the shore have come face-to-face more than sixty times.

But don't scream in terror (or close this book) just yet. Most sharks are not dangerous to humans and don't see people as prey. When a rare attack does happen, it's often because a shark confuses a splashing swimmer or surfer with an animal it usually eats, like fish or seals.

Considering more than ten million people swim and boat here each year, your odds of encountering a shark on the Jersey Shore remain incredibly low. In fact, you are more likely to be struck by lightning—or have your grumpy math teacher cancel homework for an entire month—than be bitten by a shark.

That doesn't mean shark attacks aren't

scary—they are. (And warning: so are some of the stories in this book!) But sharks are not the vicious monsters that movies and the media would have you believe. In reality, sharks are complex and curious creatures that help keep the ocean healthy and strong. Fewer than fifteen people die annually from shark-related injuries, while humans kill *millions* of sharks worldwide each year. So, maybe sharks should be more afraid of us . . . than we are of them?

In *Jaws of the Jersey Shore*, you will read the true stories of real people who have come face-to-face with sharks down the shore. Some of these people lived to tell the tale, and others, tragically, were not so lucky. Some were only swimming, boating, or fishing when a shark came calling. Others learned the hard way that it is never smart to tease, harass, or injure a wild animal—*especially* a shark.

A few stories may make you sad, others will give you a giggle, and perhaps one or two may even give you goosebumps. You'll learn more about the sharks that frequent the Jersey Shore and better understand why sharks behave the way they do. You will see why sharks' reputation as bad guys is really a bad rap for one of the ocean's most important creatures, and why sharks need our protection now more than ever. You can even check out some lifeguard-approved safety tips for Jersey Shore beachgoers that might keep a shark from spoiling *your* day at the beach. Just remember, when you wade into the waters of the Jersey Shore, you are entering a shark's home. So, swim—and read on—at your own risk!

FISHING WITH YOUR FEET IN THE SAND!

Do you like to catch fish? If you do, New Jersey is the perfect state for you. You can catch fish in freshwater ponds and streams or cruise the nearby ocean waters for game fish. Perhaps you like to catch fish with your feet firmly planted on the shore. If so, then you may love surf fishing.

Surf fishermen stand in the shallow water and

cast their lines into the deeper surf, hoping to catch a fish, such as a bluefish or a striped bass. Anytime a fisherman stands in shallow water, he must watch out for sharks. After all, fishing attracts sharks! Sometimes, an attack comes as a total surprise, like when a shark goes after a fisherman's line. Other times, people wading in shallow water bully the shark, cruelly teasing, annoying, or even harming it. When a shark feels it is under attack, it is just like you and me. It will fight to protect itself!

One June afternoon in 1966, two teenagers learned that lesson the hard way. Harry and Will were spending the day along the shore in Brigantine. They brought their fishing rods, clam rakes, and the lunches their mothers had packed. They didn't have any luck fishing, so they decided to dig up a few clams.

They were wading in less than two feet of water when they saw a large, dark-colored fish struggling in the shallows. They watched it for a while and realized it was a shark! Harry ventured closer and speared it with his rake. Although it thrashed and squirmed, the wounded animal could not get free.

They were dragging the injured shark behind them as they walked along the edge of the water when Harry's leg came too close to the mouth of the frenzied animal. It grabbed a hold of his calf with its razor-sharp teeth. Harry kicked and screamed until the shark finally let go.

When the boys saw the blood spewing from the nasty gashes on Harry's leg, they dropped the rake and left the dying shark on the beach. Will helped Harry make it to a nearby wharf and asked a local fisherman to call for help.

Harry's day of fishing ended in the hospital where he received seven stitches to close the wound left by the tormented shark. In this case, the shark didn't attack Harry; it was only trying to defend itself.

Another story comes from Egg Harbor, where in 2011, Eric and Ryan spent their free time surf-fishing near the inlet. When they heard that the striped bass were biting, they dropped what they were doing and raced to the beach. Dressed like all the other fishermen, they wore heavy waders and boots as they entered the waist-high surf.

They had only been there a few minutes when something grabbed on to Eric's leg, and he let out a yelp. He stumbled forward but somehow kept from falling into the water. He bolted for the beach with Ryan close on his heels.

When the boys looked more closely, they found a set of large teeth marks on Eric's pant leg. Shark teeth! No one knew what kind of shark had grabbed him, but they did know that Eric needed a new pair of waders.

Shark attacks can happen when you least expect them. Vincent didn't expect to meet a shark when he arrived on Sandy Hook one October morning in 1975. He was thinking about the giant fish he might catch.

Yanking his waders and fishing tackle from the back of his car, Vincent tramped across the beach until he reached the water's edge. He was holding his surf pole in his left hand as he waded slowly into the chilly water. Just as he was about to cast his line into the deeper water, there was a loud splash.

11

At that moment, something grabbed ahold of his right leg and jerked Vincent off his feet. Still holding on to his rod, Vincent kicked and yelled with all his might. He rammed his rod into the sand, pushed on it to get to his feet, and headed to the shore. He didn't look back to see if whatever had grabbed him was still there until he was safely on the beach.

Vincent stood there for a few minutes trying to catch his breath. He couldn't see what had pulled him into the deeper water and didn't know he was injured until he looked down. To his shock, blood was oozing from a large jagged rip in his waders.

The park rangers rushed him to a local hospital where doctors stitched and bandaged his seven-inch wound. Although he was injured, it wasn't long before Vincent was back on the beach trying to catch a giant-sized bluefish.

Another way to fish with your feet in the sand is to rake clams or dig for oysters, like Harry and Will at Brigantine. Although most of the clams and oysters we eat are caught by boat, many people like to find the hidden shellfish themselves.

Clams can be found on the sandy beaches along inlets and coves where the water is less salty than the open ocean. Oysters like salty water, so fishermen need to dig in slightly deeper depths to find the sweet eastern oyster that is so famous in New Jersey. Regardless of where shell fishermen are hunting, they need to keep an eye out for roving sharks that might be attracted to all the commotion.

Although it was long ago, people are still

talking about one famous shark attack in 1886, where no fewer than three unruly sharks attacked two men gathering clams near Highlands.

It started out like any normal day. John and Edward were gathering clams in the shallow areas of the Shrewsbury Inlet, which once connected the Shrewsbury River to the Atlantic Ocean. (The inlet is now closed and the Shrewsbury River connects to Sandy Hook Bay.) John and Edward were standing in about four feet of water, raking clams, when three sets of jagged jaws zeroed in on them without warning. Although the men beat on the sharks' snouts, the flashing teeth and snapping jaws came within inches of their faces.

John and Edward scrambled into their nearby rowboat and thought they were safe. But the sharks stayed close. They swam circles around the boat, getting closer each time until their teeth scraped the wooden hull.

Then, one shark rammed the rowboat, sending it sideways across the water! Before it came to rest, another shark butted it again and the boat spun around once more. The men tried to keep the curious sharks away by slamming their heads with oars until they heard the sound of wood splintering. Soon, to their horror, drops of water began to seep into the bottom of the boat.

The men tried to row as quickly as they could for the nearest shore. When they looked back, the sharks were close behind. Flashing their razor-sharp teeth, the sharks inched nearer and nearer to their boat. It wasn't until the boat reached the beach that the sharks ended their pursuit and swam away. Thankfully, no one was hurt that day—that is, except for the little rowboat.

Oystermen also sometimes come face-to-face with sharks when they least expect it. In this case, three teenage brothers were raking oysters in the shallow waters of Delaware Bay in 1907. They were standing in waist-high water with their rowboat anchored nearby. It had been a successful day, and their baskets were nearly full. The youngest brother, Georgie, yanked his rake from the water and leaned forward to look at the tiny oysters. Just then, he was sideswiped by a large dark creature that knocked him off his feet. George slipped underwater but instantly popped back up, holding his chest with both hands.

When the shark moved to strike again, George's brothers took charge, armed with their heavy rakes. One brother shoved Georgie into the boat while the others shouted and hammered on the shark until it turned away. Everyone jumped on board and they rowed away as fast as they could.

Georgie was still holding his chest when they reached the shore. Although the shark had left a large scrape across his chest, the wound was not bleeding. He was treated by a doctor and sent home to rest. From that day on, his brothers often teased him by making kissing noises and claiming that he had been kissed by a shark, but Georgie never got mad. He said that it was better to be kissed by a shark than to be eaten by one.

You will not likely meet up with a shark when you are fishing or clamming along the Jersey Shore. But it could happen. After all, when we go into the ocean, we are in the shark's backyard. It is up to us to keep ourselves safe.

SWIMMERS, SURFERS, AND THE SHARKS THEY MEET

Who do you think is most likely to be bitten by a shark? Would it be a fisherman, a swimmer, or a surfer? If you guessed that a swimmer or surfer would be in the most danger, you would be wrong. Although millions of people swim in the waters along New Jersey's shore each year, very few come face-to-face with a shark. Shark attacks are so uncommon that only sixty have been reported in the last two hundred years. In all that time, only fourteen have been swimmers or surfers.

Although shark attacks do not happen very often, even a simple shark bite can be serious. As long as lifeguards are present, swimming from our beaches along the shore is safe. Yet, entering the water *without* lifeguards on duty is both foolish and dangerous. Not only are lifeguards trained to save you from drowning but they can also spot sharks before they come too close. Don't fool around when lifeguards give the signal to leave the water. When they stand on their chairs, blow their whistles, and wave their arms in the "come here" motion, get out of the water!

A teenager who was swimming in the ocean

at Seaside Park in 1926 learned that lesson the hard way. Charles and his buddies were having a great time. They were all good swimmers, and they swam out to the sandbar beyond the breakers. They were fooling around, laughing and splashing one another. Just then, the warning whistles screeched across the beachfront. The lifeguards had spotted a shark! The blare of the whistles never stopped as every guard on the beach leaped to the top of his tower and frantically waved people from the water. Sadly, Charles and his pals didn't pay attention to the whistle or signals before it was too late.

Within seconds, a blood-curdling scream echoed across the water as a shark latched on to Charles's arm. One friend reached toward him, but at that moment, the shark plunged to the depths with Charles in tow. Although the lifeguards raced to the spot, and beachgoers searched the beach for many hours, Charles could not be found. Several days later, his body—missing its head, arms, and one leg—was found washed up on a nearby beach.

A few decades earlier in 1902, a man only known as Harry was swimming in the ocean in Atlantic City when he saw a large dark form floating in the water. He thought it might be someone drowning, so he raced to the spot and grabbed it with both hands. He saw his mistake right away, but it was too late. He was holding on to the tail of a large shark.

The startled animal whirled about and tried to latch on to Harry's foot. Harry dodged the attack and began swimming for shore as fast as he could, with the shark close on his heels. But the shark was a faster swimmer than Harry. Its giant teeth ripped flesh and muscle from his left arm, turning the water red.

The lifeguards rushed to his aid and killed the shark with their harpoons. Doctors were able to treat Harry's wounds. They healed, leaving him with long, ragged scars. The species of shark that attacked Harry that day is still a mystery.

Paul, another Atlantic City man, loved to swim in deep ocean water farther away from the crowded beaches. He often took charter fishing boats that traveled several miles offshore and then would pay the captain to let him dive into the deep water and swim while the others were fishing.

One August day in 1905, Paul jumped into the water from the bow of the ship as the others were casting their fishing lines into the water at the stern (rear of the boat). A few minutes later, the captain saw two dark shadows moving through the water toward Paul.

The captain signaled to return to the boat, but Paul did not take it seriously enough. He slowly began swimming toward the boat, unaware of the two sharks getting closer and closer. Soon, everyone on board was shouting and waving to Paul to swim faster. By the time he saw the danger, it was too late. One of the sharks bit down on his foot. At that moment, the captain fired his gun, and the sharks disappeared into the sea. When they dragged Paul back onto the boat, blood was gushing from where he once had toes. Although a shark had bitten off three of his toes, Paul survived. He walked with a limp for the rest of his life but never gave up deep-water swimming.

Both Ocean City and Surf City are popular surfing spots. In July of 1980, a young surfer tried to do a somersault into a wave when something struck his back, leaving a round wound that required sixty stitches. Because a shark was not sighted, some said he must have hit a piece of driftwood in the water. Soon afterward, however, another surfer was struck by an unidentified creature. More than forty stitches were needed to close his wound.

Shark attacks are scary. Most people who see an attack are often so upset by the bloody wounds that they don't remember much else. Sometimes, no one remembers seeing a shark at the scene at all; if they do, few can describe it well enough to identify the culprit.

rk, of the Man-Eating Species, Caught at Belfort, N. J.

A Man-Eating Female Shark Which Was Caught Off Bel
terday in a Net After a Terrible Battle. The Shark
a Quarter Feet in Length and Weighed 215 Pounds.
Was Cut Open Twelve Baby Sharks, Each Eightee
Were Found.

Head of the Man-Eating Monster, Showing Its Massive Jaws and
Teeth. Some Idea of the Size of the Shark's Head Can Be Formed
by a Comparison of the Heads of the Men Who Are Standing Nearby.

OVERNMENT TO AID
FIGHT TO STAMP OUT
THE SHARK HORROR

ll Out Coast Guard
to Hunt Man-eaters

The United States Government
declared war on the sharks

Cabinet Meeting Pre-
cedes Federal Ac-

THREE DIE OF HEAT
BEFORE COOL WIND
TUMBLES MERCURY

Thermometer   Drops
Thirteen Degrees in Five
Hours

Change of Breeze to East at
Night, However, Brings With
It Increased Humidity

CARRANZA [
WISH WAR
READY TO E

Reforms to
ated in Me
tution Shor

Presidential Ele
construction
and on a Fir

1916: SHARK TERROR ON THE SHORE

Whenever people talk about shark attacks at the Jersey Shore, they usually talk about the tragedy that took place in Matawan, New Jersey, over a hundred years ago. It was a grisly attack in which four people lost their lives and five more were injured, and people are still talking about it today.

What many people do not know is that the tragedy at Matawan on July 12, 1916, was not the first shark attack on the shore that month, and it would not be the last. Humans and sharks would come face-to-face more often between June 30 and July 12 than ever before in U.S. history. The attacks began in Atlantic City and moved steadily northward for two weeks. It would not end until July 12, in the murky waters of Matawan Creek.

THE FIRST ATTACK: JUNE 30, ATLANTIC CITY, NJ

The two weeks of terror began in the southern part of the Jersey Shore in the resort town of Atlantic City. June 30 was a beautiful summer day, and the beaches were full of happy swimmers.

One was a twelve-year-old boy making the most of his last vacation day at the shore. He was diving in and out of the breakers and didn't see the large dark fin speeding straight for him. By the time he realized he was in trouble, it was too late. He swam for shore as fast as he could, but he could not outswim the shark.

Razor-sharp jaws clamped down on his leg like a giant pair of pliers. Then, as quickly as it attacked, the shark let go and disappeared. The lifeguards heard the boy's screams, quickly pulled him from the water, and tried to stop the bleeding.

The boy's injuries were serious. He was rushed to the hospital, where doctors found all the flesh peeled away from his heel and foot. It was a bloody and painful wound, but he did recover.

The summer didn't start well for this young man, but he survived to swim another day. The story of the attack didn't make the newspapers, so no one was prepared for what happened the very next day.

THE SECOND ATTACK: JULY 1, BEACH HAVEN NJ - 20 MILES NORTH OF ATLANTIC CITY

That first day of July was hot and humid. Like many others on the train from Philadelphia to Beach Haven that day, a doctor with his son and daughter were headed to cool off by the coast. His son, Charles, was so eager to go swimming that he didn't wait for his father or sister. While they unpacked for their week-long stay, Charles changed into his swim trunks and raced to the nearest beach. When his family arrived at the beach, they found Charles standing in the surf playing with a dog. He waved to them, turned, and raced into the coming waves. He swam away from the shore into the deeper water beyond the breakers.

Within minutes, a blood-curdling scream echoed across the beach. The lifeguards leaped from their chairs and raced toward the direction of the outcry. By the time they reached Charles, he was thrashing about wildly within a circle of red water.

They grabbed him and began to tow him back to shore, but a shark had sunk its teeth into Charles and would not let go. It held on to the bloody swimmer until they reached shallow water. In an instant, the shark disappeared.

Other swimmers rushed to help the guards bring Charles back to shore. His father, who had watched the attack from the beach, rushed to his side. Although he was a medical doctor, he could not save his son's life. The wounds were too severe. Charles had been in Beach Haven for less than two hours, and now he was dead.

Word spread quickly, so the hotels along the shore put on extra lifeguards. Others strung underwater wire fencing around their beaches to keep out the sharks. This was the first fatal shark attack of the summer. But it would not be the last.

THE THIRD ATTACK: JULY 6, SPRING LAKE, NJ

Just five days later, on July 6, a shark attack would once again claim a victim. This time it would take place in Spring Lake, just thirty-two miles north of Beach Haven. Spring Lake has been a popular vacation destination for many years. One of the most famous hotels at the time was the Essex and Sussex Hotel, located just feet from the beach. It was the end of the Fourth of July weekend, and the hotel was full of guests. These were the days before TV or radio, so not many knew about the attack in Beach Haven the previous day.

The Spring Lake victim was a young Swiss man, Charles Bruder, who worked as a bellhop at the hotel. It was such a hot day that when he finally got his break in the middle of the afternoon, he headed straight for the beach for a quick cooling swim.

Charles was athletic and a strong swimmer, so he had no problem swimming out about a hundred yards from the beach. Suddenly, a sound between a scream and a yelp echoed across the beach. The lifeguards spotted him thrashing about wildly in the middle of a widening circle of red water.

When the rescue boats reached Charles, he was still alive. They stretched out an oar for him to grab, but he could not hold on. Just as they were pulling him onto the boat, the shark struck again. Charles screamed, "It bit off my legs!" and passed out at the bottom of the boat.

They raced back to shore as fast as they could, but by the time they reached the beach, Charles had died. His wounds were ghastly. One leg was bitten off between the ankle and knee, leaving a bloody ragged stump. The other leg was missing the foot altogether, and the bones between the knee and foot were crushed within a bloody mass of tissue and torn blood vessels. There was even a giant gash across his stomach that spewed blood across the sand. Efforts to save him were unsuccessful.

Word of the attack spread like wildfire. This time, the shark attack made national news. After a few days, however, reports of the attacks were off the front page. People thought the summer of sharks was over, but the worst was yet to come. Six days later, a day of true shark terror would rock the Jersey Shore.

THE FOURTH ATTACK: JULY 12, MATAWAN

On July 12, 1916, sharks were the last thing on peoples' minds in Matawan. The little town is eight miles inland from the ocean. Its muddy creek winds its way through the wetlands and marshes until it reaches the shore near Keyport. No one could have ever predicted that before the day was over, two people would be dead, and five more injured by a shark.

The first attack of the day took the life of a twelve-year-old boy named Lester Stillwell. Like many boys his age, he worked part-time with his father at a nearby basket factory. On this day, he worked until lunchtime and then raced to meet his pals who were already swimming in Matawan Creek.

Lester hung his clothes on a nearby bush and jumped into the water. He stretched out and let his body float on the surface before shouting, "Hey! Watch me float!" For a few minutes, everything was quiet.

Then something beneath the water brushed against one of his pals, who thought it was an old piece of wood floating in the creek. He turned around just in time to watch as the strange-shaped timber suddenly sped forward and rammed Lester, knocking him into the air. As Lester fell back into the water, the boys saw a great fin appear. The huge white underbelly flashed for just a second as its oversized pointed teeth sank into Lester's body. There was an ear-piercing scream followed by a gurgle as Lester vanished beneath the surface of Matawan

Creek. The boys raced from the water, screaming all the way to Main Street.

Arthur Smith, Red Burlew, and Stanley Fisher heard the shouting and raced to the creek bank. Lester was not in sight. They peeled off their clothes and dove into the murky brown water searching for the missing boy. Time after time, they plunged into the water to continue their search. After a few minutes, they would pop back to the surface just long enough to take a deep breath. Then, once again, they nose-dived into the creek and continued their search.

People quickly gathered along the waterfront, including Lester's parents. He had been missing for over half an hour, and Stanley knew they were running out of time. When he saw the blood in the water, he feared the worst. Although Stanley knew it was likely too late, he continued to dive into the creek, over and over again. He could not give up the search with Lester's weeping parents standing there watching.

Just then, one of the other rescuers, Arthur Smith, bolted to the surface. He yelped in pain, shouting that he had been whacked by something with sandpaper-like skin. The water around him turned a murky red as he made his way to shore. Although his wound required first aid, he was not seriously injured. The shark had sideswiped him.

Stanley dove into the water once more. This time, he spotted the body near the bottom. Just as he grabbed ahold of the boy, a mouth of razor-sharp teeth latched on to his thigh. He broke the surface of the water screaming at the top of his lungs. People on the creek bank watched in horror as he fought for his life against the shark. The water all around Stanley was like red soapsuds as the shark continued its attack. Others on nearby boats rushed to help, banging on the beast with their oars until it finally let go of Stanley. They pulled the bleeding rescuer onto the boat and raced to the shore. Although his injuries were severe, Stanley was alert, talking with his rescuers about what had happened.

While the local doctor was trying to save Stanley's life, another group of teens were happily swimming in the creek farther downstream, unaware of what had just happened. They heard raised voices and then someone shouting, "*Shark!*"

The boys scrambled from the water one by one, climbing the ladder onto the dock. Joseph

Dunn was last in line. Just as he stepped on the first rung, something yanked him back into the creek. He screamed and fought whatever had a hold of him. His brother jumped into the creek and tried to free him from the shark's grasp. A nearby fisherman saw the uproar and raced to help.

Although he wasn't as critically injured as Stanley, Joseph had serious wounds. There were no crushed bones or torn arteries, but his left leg was cut to ribbons from his knee to his ankle. A local man watching the rescue efforts offered to drive the boy to New Brunswick for medical care. Joseph survived the thirty-mile car ride to the hospital but would be a patient there for the next sixty days.

Meanwhile, Stanley Fisher was still stretched out on the nearby shore waiting to be taken to

JAWS OF THE JERSEY SHORE

the hospital. It was several hours later, after he arrived in Long Branch, that he died. Stanley had tried to save the young boy's life but ended up losing his own.

Talk of the shark attacks flew across Matawan. People came with harpoons, spears, clubs, axes, and shotguns, determined to destroy the beast that had killed the boy and his would-be rescuer. They even took all the dynamite from the hardware store and tried to blow up anything lurking in the creek. The shark was never caught.

Some say this was the end of the shark attacks that summer. But we know that on July 13, the day after the heartbreaking events in Matawan, there were three more shark incidents nearby.

Sheepshead Bay, New York, is just eight miles from where Matawan Creek enters the ocean. On the morning of July 13, two swimmers came face-to-face with a shark. One frightened away her attacker by shouting and smacking the water with her hands. The other managed to leap into a nearby rowboat the minute he heard someone shout, "Shark!"

On that same morning, in these same waters, a small fishing boat from Sea Bright was suddenly rammed by a large shark. It knocked the three men into the water. With the shark hovering nearby, they managed to upright the boat and scramble inside.

The two weeks of shark terror finally came to an end. Although it happened over a century ago, people still talk and write about it more than any other Jersey Shore shark attack. Some argue it was the work of a single shark that swam northward from Atlantic City to the New York waters. Others claim it had to be more than one shark. Many people believe it was the work of a bull shark, known for its aggressiveness and tolerance for brackish water. (Brackish water is when salty seawater mixes with freshwater, usually where the ocean meets inland water creeks, such as rivers, ponds, and lakes.) Others insist that only a white shark could do that kind of damage.

We may never know what kind of shark attacked our shore that summer. Nor are we likely to know if the tragic events were carried out by a single shark or if there was more than one culprit. And we will most likely never learn why they attacked these swimmers on our beaches.

We only know that the Jersey Shore was the site of a series of vicious shark attacks that terrorized locals for two weeks back in 1916.

HAVE YOU EVER SEEN A FLYING SHARK?

Have you ever seen a flying shark? If you are like most people, you'll say that sharks can't fly. But if you look back at the history of shark attacks here at the Jersey Shore, you will find several surprising reports of when sharks *did*, in fact, fly!

It was the summer of 1935 when the trawler,

Nautilus, with its five-man crew, arrived at the fishing banks. As they dropped their nets into the deep waters just offshore of Wildwood, there was a loud clunking sound, and the motor ground to a halt.

Captain Chador was an experienced sailor and knew immediately that there was a block in the cable just below the water line. It wasn't a complicated problem, but it had to be repaired before they could continue their work. He ordered the small landing boat lowered to the surface of the water. Then he grabbed ahold of the rope ladder and climbed down.

The captain shoved away from the side of the *Nautilus* and let the boat drift a few feet before he picked up the oars and began to row. It was then that he caught a glimpse of a giant fin speeding straight for him.

Before he could shout out to his crew, the huge gray shark soared into the air. It sailed overhead and even seemed to hang there for just a moment. Then it suddenly dropped from the sky and landed with a giant wallop across the width of his small boat. There was the sound of splintering wood as the boat suddenly lurched sideways across the water.

The giant shark thrashed and convulsed every which way, pinning the skipper against the side of the boat. It curled its great snout toward him, snapping its jagged teeth in the captain's face. Although the captain banged on its huge gray head with his fists, the shark continued its attack.

Captain Chador let out a piercing scream

as razor-sharp teeth sliced through his skin in one long gash from the upper arm to the wrist. Then, there was a second scream as the shark bit off four of the captain's fingers.

Finally, a crewman planted a harpoon deep into the shark's head. The animal jerked backward and fell into the sea. The little boat rolled on its side, flinging the captain into the water.

Two crewmen jumped in and pulled him to safety. The first mate took command, and the *Nautilus* raced back to port with their injured captain. He was treated at the hospital, where he received dozens of stitches to close the wounds on his arm. The remaining stubs of his fingers were cleaned and bandaged.

Some reports about flying sharks can make you laugh, especially when the fisherman who claimed to catch the shark wasn't even holding a fishing rod. The *Bingo III* was a well-equipped fishing boat that often took paying passengers deep-sea fishing off the coast of Brielle, New Jersey. On this hot July day in 1941, the boat was set to take two Philadelphia men fishing for tuna.

When the men arrived, the captain knew at once they were not experienced fishermen. Unlike most fishermen, who dress in old shirts and jeans, the two men were dressed for a day at the office. They wore pale blue dress shirts and dark slacks. Instead of sneakers or fishing boots, they wore newly shined leather loafers.

Michael carried a large picnic hamper, a thermos, and a big colorful sun hat. Likewise, his friend Rick dragged two zebra-striped deck chairs and an oversized tote bag that kept falling off his shoulder. The captain knew his crew would need to give the two a great deal of help if they were to catch anything during this trip.

Although the crew tried to teach Michael and Rick how to catch a tuna, the two were more interested in setting up their chairs and picnic hampers in a spot where they had a good view of the water.

They were well on their way to the fishing grounds when the deckhand gave them fishing rods and tried to show them how to cast into the water, set the hook, and reel in the line. The men listened carefully, tried to do it once or twice, but then laid the poles down at the base of their chairs and opened up their picnic hampers.

The captain gave the order to cast lines and the two men gently tossed their lines into the water before returning to their deck chairs. Just then, a large gray shark charged the boat. Before anyone could speak, the shark launched itself into the air. The huge gray mass hung motionless for a split second. Then it dropped from the sky and landed directly in Michael's lap.

Rick was knocked off his chair as Michael and the 185-pound mako shark crashed onto the deck. The crew yanked Michael away from the shark's jagged teeth just in time. As the convulsing shark slammed its giant body toward anything in its sight, a crewman quickly steered the two inexperienced fishermen to safety. Once the shark was dead, Rick grabbed their camera and began taking pictures.

As the boat pulled into port, the men thanked the captain for such an exciting adventure. Michael was delighted that he had caught such a massive shark on his first fishing trip. No one had the heart to tell him that he didn't catch the shark. The flying shark had caught him!

In another case, two men were fishing for bluefish in the waters off Long Branch when, suddenly, a shark landed in their boat.

Jason had just hooked a large bluefish and was struggling to reel it to the surface. Just as he first glimpsed the fish, a huge dark fin streaked toward the boat. Before he could speak, there was a giant thud, the little boat shuddered, and Jason dropped his fishing rod.

A massive gray shark soared over the back of the boat and crashed onto the deck. The uninvited guest stretched across the middle of the boat, with Jason trapped in the rear and his friend Saul in the front.

The angry beast thrust its huge jagged teeth

toward the men as if urging them to come closer as it slammed its huge tail back and forth against the side of the boat. Each blow was accompanied by the sound of splintering wood.

Jason and Saul knew they had to do something. The frame of the boat was weakening with each smack of the shark's massive tail. If the wood gave way, the boat would sink, and they were miles from shore. If they didn't act soon, they would both drown.

Jason grabbed an ax and Saul picked up the bluefish bat. After a few sharp blows to the snout, the uninvited shark lay motionless at the bottom of the boat. Although they hadn't caught a single bluefish, they did have a five-hundred-pound shark to take to the market and a fisherman's tale of the day they caught the flying shark.

WHO SAID YOU CAN'T CATCH A SHARK WITH A NET?

If you ask any Jersey Shore fisherman, he will tell you that if you want to catch a shark you need a rod and reel. You would never use a net if you wanted to snag such a heavy fish. That makes sense, but we know that every year tens of thousands of sharks are killed when they get caught in fishing nets. Although this is never

done on purpose, sharks do get caught this way.
Neither sharks nor humans are happy when this
happens.

Fishermen know that when a shark gets
caught in their nets it will cost them money. It
may eat or scare away their catch or damage or
destroy their costly equipment. Likewise, sharks
are frightened when they are trapped inside a
fishing net. They are swimming along searching
for smaller fish to eat, and they do not see the
huge net closing them inside before it is too late.
All that is left for the shark to do is fight for
its life.

This is likely what happened in the summer
of 1886 when Captain White met not one, but
four very angry sharks caught in his fishing net.
The captain and his two-man crew had been
fishing for small baitfish known as mossbunkers

most of the day. If they were lucky, they would have a big haul of the tiny silvery fish, which would be a good payday for everyone.

Captain White gave the order to haul in the nets. The gears groaned as the net slowly began to rise from the water. Suddenly, there was a loud clang at the rear of the boat. The winch that lifted the net from the water jammed, and the boat trembled and lurched forward.

The crew ran to the rear of the boat. Their eyes popped when they saw the sharks thrashing wildly in their net. The men grabbed any weapons they could find and began beating on the trapped animals. The giant wiggling mass of gray flesh lunged toward the crewmen with huge jagged teeth that snapped wildly in the air while their giant tails hammered the side of the boat. Finally, the nets gave way. The four sharks

JAWS OF THE JERSEY SHORE

and the day's catch dropped into the sea. The day's catch was lost, the nets were ruined, but no one was hurt.

Although the temperatures were below zero on New Year's Day in 1923, a fishing boat from Ocean City was netting for cod in icy offshore waters. The seas were choppy, and a bitter wind blew the sea spray into icicles that clung to the crew's hair and formed a solid layer of ice on their oilskin coats. There was a sigh of relief when the captain gave the order to draw in the nets. That meant they could finish their work and get inside where it was warm.

But suddenly, the winch grunted to a stop. The bulging net swung back and forth at the back of the boat. There was a loud cracking sound and the boat shuddered as the entire net crashed onto the deck. Thousands of silvery floppy fish spilled in every direction. Still tangled within the net was one very large and angry shark.

The crew bolted away from the frightened animal as it heaved itself from side to side, all the while flashing its mouthful of huge jagged teeth. Its great tail slammed one way and then the other, sending most of the day's catch back into the water.

Some crew ran for weapons while others grabbed nearby rope. They made a lasso and were trying to tie down its tail when it jerked sideways, hitting a crewman and breaking his leg. Others who tried to bind its jaws received cuts, bruises, and scratches.

After a long struggle, the shark was finally killed. The crew gave one another first aid for their injuries, and the dead shark was rolled into the sea. They retrieved as much of their catch as they could, hoping it would be enough to pay for the damaged net.

Years later, on a November day in 1928, three cod fishermen were offshore in their sixteen-foot Jersey skiff. Instead of codfish, two large bull sharks got trapped in their tiny net. It was a fishing trip the men would never forget.

The Sea Bright fishermen were up early that day. They left their homes before dawn and were ready to net for cod by the time the sun rose. They gently dropped their net into the water and slowly dragged it along the skiff.

They had not traveled far before the boat suddenly shifted to the side as if the net was full of fish. The men couldn't believe their good luck. Had the nets filled so quickly? The trio began to pull in the net hand over hand as carefully as they could. They didn't want any of the precious cod to escape. At first, there were only a few fish, and then one of the men bellowed, "Shark!"

Just then, an oversized tail reached from the water and slammed against the side of the boat. The sound of cracking wood echoed around them as their small skiff shook and wobbled uncontrollably. When the men peered into the net, all they saw were two sharks staring back at them. The skiff shimmied and shook, bouncing across the water as the two giants thrashed, rammed, and hammered on the hull of the boat. Giant teeth snapped ever closer to the men's faces as they fought to keep the skiff afloat.

The men knew they had to do something. If the boat sank, they would be at the mercy of the sharks. While the captain tried to keep the boat afloat, the other two men beat and stabbed the angry animals using anything they could find. But these sharks were not giving up easily.

The battle went on for two hours before the sharks, entangled in the netting, lay motionless alongside the boat. By then, the men were exhausted, sweaty, and bloody. But the job was not done. Once they were certain the sharks were dead, the dog-tired men had to carefully untangle their bodies from the precious net. Working carefully so they didn't damage the net further, they eventually freed the sharks' bodies and headed back to shore.

When the men finally reached the dock, they rushed to check the damage. It wasn't until they knew the net could be repaired that they finally got first aid for their injuries.

The three men felt lucky. They had not

been seriously injured, their boat had survived, and their net could be repaired. That meant they would soon be back on the water fishing for cod. Although the men didn't say it, they were relieved that the two bull sharks would no longer roam their cod fishing waters and bother unsuspecting fishermen.

WHEN SHARKS ATTACK BOATS!

We do not know why sharks sometimes attack boats without warning. It would make sense that a shark might strike back if the boat somehow injured or frightened it. But most of these attacks on boats and ships come without warning. In most cases, an aggressive shark suddenly appears, attacking the boat and the people on board.

Some people believe that sharks think boats are invading their territory. Thousands of boats travel shark-filled waters each day, and yet there are only a few such attacks each year. Others say that sharks may think fishing boats are stealing their food source. Could that be true? Or perhaps the noisy engines or smells of marine paint and varnish foul the water so much that the sharks feel under attack.

Usually, a shark about to attack a boat will swim around it two or three times. With each circle, the shark gets closer and closer to the boat until it is nearly rubbing up against the sides of the watercraft. The shark may seem to disappear for a minute or two, and then it will charge the boat at full speed, ramming it with its massive snout.

Newspapers do not always print stories about sharks that attack fishing boats. But this account in 1926 made headlines along the Jersey Shore. It wasn't because people were seriously injured or because their boat was destroyed. It was such a big deal because the attacker was a shark seldom spotted here at the Jersey Shore. It was a seven-foot-long thresher shark!

The two fishermen, Andrew and Peter, were in the Army together for several years. They loved fishing together, so when they left the Army, they bought an old fishing boat named the *Mary Sue*. They never went far from shore but always managed to bring home a nice pile of fish for their families. On this day, they found a good spot not far from Sea Bright and dropped their anchor. They baited and cast their lines and then sat down to wait.

It was Andrew who first spotted the shark when it made a wide loop around their boat. When the shark made its next circle, Andrew saw that it was very unusual. The shark was grayish-brown with a long sickle-shaped tail that looked to be even longer than its snout. He couldn't believe his eyes because it was a thresher shark! Threshers are shy animals seldom seen in shallow waters, and they're known to avoid human contact. Andrew had never before seen a living thresher shark on the Jersey Shore.

The men stared wide-eyed at the thresher as it swam circles around their boat. Each time it passed, it came nearer and nearer. They were laughing about the shark's strange behavior when, in a sudden burst of speed, it charged the *Mary Sue*. At the very last minute, the shark dived deeper, slapping the back of the boat with its giant sickle-shaped tail. The boat shuddered and lurched sideways.

Before they could react, the shark was back again, ramming the side of their boat. Wood splintered, and their bucket of bait fish spilled across the deck. Their food basket toppled over, sandwiches and snacks mixing with a gooey slosh of squirming fish.

No one had to say a word. Andrew lifted the anchor as Peter gunned the engine, moving the *Mary Sue* as far away from the shark as quickly as possible. Andrew kept one eye out for traces of water seeping into the boat while Peter watched for any sign of the thresher. The *Mary Sue* didn't suffer serious damage, and the men lost only their lunch and their bait. Both the fishermen and the thresher shark lived to meet another day.

One of the earliest reports of a shark attack on a boat was reported in a local newspaper over a hundred and thirty years ago. In those days, before electric fans or air conditioning, people did whatever they could to keep cool on a hot summer day. Often, people would hitch a ride with a friendly boat owner and cruise along the shore, enjoying the afternoon sea breeze. That is exactly how our next story came to pass.

Four friends were on their buddy's fishing boat one hot August afternoon. The boat headed toward Sandy Hook Bay. The captain was at the wheel while the others stretched out on the deck, their faces to the wind. Sharks were the last thing on their minds.

At first, all they saw was a dark shadow just below the surface of the water that slowly circled their boat. They were debating what sort of creature it might be when it suddenly broke away from the circle, spurt through the water, and rammed the bottom of their boat.

All the men could do was hold on as the boat rose above the water and then slammed back down with a loud wallop. Water sprayed everywhere, and their belongings spewed across the deck. Before they could react, the shark was back again. This time, it slammed the side of the boat! The men grabbed whatever they could get their hands on and began beating on the beast's snout. Although it was outnumbered four to one, the seven-foot bull shark put up a fight the men would not soon forget. They finally hauled the shark on board and headed back to shore to show off their trophy. They reported that no one was injured, although the shark might disagree.

The result was very different on a Jersey Shore fishing boat during a shark attack back in June of 1880. Although no one was killed, the boat nearly sank, a crewman was washed overboard, and the crew was forced to serve nearly half of

their catch to a determined and *very* hungry shark.

It had been a good day on the water, and by noon, the hatches were full with eight hundred pounds of fresh fish. The crew lifted anchor and were bound for the fish market onshore when the first mate, David, saw a large creature following them. He shouted to the captain that a really large dolphin was following the boat. But the moment the captain saw it, he knew it was a shark.

It followed them for a bit and then suddenly raced toward them, ramming the boat full force with its head. Water gushed in through the ragged hole along the water line.

The chaos really began when the shark's head got stuck. The shark thrust its body upwards and downward, jerking sideways and heaving its great body back and forth. But no matter what the shark did, its huge head remained wedged in the bottom of the boat.

The boat was bobbing up and down as it bounced sideways across the water. In an instant, David lost his grip and flew overboard. Splashing and sputtering for air, he knew he had to get back on board before the shark got loose— or he was a goner. Time and again, he tried but failed to catch hold. Finally, using every ounce of his strength, David hurled his body alongside the boat and was able to fling himself up and over the rail. Gasping with relief, he fell onto the deck with a thud, inches from the shark's snapping jaws.

Just then, the shark yanked its head from the hole in the bottom of the boat. Water rushed in and swiftly began to rise. Now they were sinking. They were bailing water as fast as they could when another fisherman nearby saw what was happening and raced to their aid. They put a temporary plug in the hole of the boat and bailed out all the seawater.

They were still nearly a mile from shore and were not out of danger. They sped for the nearest port, hoping the plug would hold till they reached the dock. They thought the worst was over until David looked back to wave goodbye to the other fishermen. He couldn't believe his eyes. There was the same shark, and it was following them!

It was closer than before, and soon it was swimming alongside them. David had to do something. He grabbed some fish from the hold and tossed them at the shark. The beast didn't even slow down as it swallowed the fish whole.

David threw fish after fish at the speeding shark. Yet it was never satisfied, coming back again and again, ever closer to the boat. He tried throwing an armful of fish to slow it down, but nothing worked.

Just as they entered Barnegat Bay, David grabbed one of the large plastic tubs and filled it with fish. He lifted it over his head and dumped it over the shark's huge snout as it came within inches of the boat. While the shark was gorging itself on the fishy feast, the boat raced into the safety of the harbor.

When they got to the fish market, their haul of eight hundred pounds of fresh fish had been reduced to only four hundred pounds. They had been forced to feed half of their catch to the shark that had tried to sink them. Although the boat was seriously damaged and required expensive repairs, neither man was seriously hurt. The shark, however, had a full belly.

SHARKS ONBOARD: NOT WELL-BEHAVED PASSENGERS

Sharks are an important part of the ocean's food chain, and we need to protect them. But we must remember that sharks do not make good playmates. Neither would they be good dinner guests. They eat raw fish and often swallow their food whole in one noisy gulp. Don't even think about taking them on a road trip unless the inside of your car is waterproof. So, it doesn't come as a surprise that sharks are seldom well-behaved whenever they are brought on board boats. In all fairness, sharks are nearly always brought on board against their will.

We read about sharks flying through the air and landing on boats in Chapter Four (Have You Ever Seen a Flying Shark?). This happens when a shark misjudges their speed and distance and ends up landing on an unsuspecting boat. Other times, sharks are going about their own business when they see yummy-looking fish that would make a perfect lunch. They go in for a nibble, and before they know it, they are snagged by a large sharp hook and being dragged through the water and yanked onto a boat. By that time, they are tired, confused, and angry. They are ready to fight. Any fisherman can tell you that having a live shark on board is more than just annoying, it is downright dangerous.

In a 1932 account from Sea Isle City, a shark brought on board in a fishing net not only caused most of their catch to escape but also injured a young crewman. The *Sea Lily* captain and two-man crew had been fishing for cod in the deep waters offshore since dawn. When the captain gave the order to haul in the nets, Antonio and Luke cheered and hurried to the back of the boat to guide the net onto the deck.

The winch groaned as it lifted the swollen mesh from the water. They swung it over the deck and released the holding knot. Hundreds of cod erupted from the hole and spilled across the deck.

Just then, the torso of a giant shark appeared in the heap of wiggling fish, only inches from the two crewmen. Fish were flopping in every direction as the giant beast, still tangled in the net, thrashed and lurched frantically trying to escape. Its huge tail swished across the deck, knocking anything in its path overboard into the sea.

Suddenly, the shark jerked sideways and sank its huge teeth into Antonio's leg. Although Antonio bellowed in pain, the shark would not let go. Luke sped to his side and plunged his knife deep into the shark's eye. Antonio's screaming never stopped as Luke jammed the knife into the shark over and over until Antonio's leg was free.

The captain cut the engine and rushed to help. He inspected Antonio's wound and quickly took off his shirt, using it to slow the bleeding. While Luke held pressure on the wound, the captain raced the *Sea Lily* to the nearest port. Antonio was rushed to a nearby hospital, but his wound was so serious he was moved to Philadelphia for advanced treatment. He survived but carried the scar his entire life.

All along our shores, charter boats are available for anyone who wants to go deep-sea fishing. People pay a fee to go out to the fishing grounds where they try their luck at catching large fish such as blues, cod, or tuna. The boats usually supply fishing gear as well as crewmembers to help those who may not know how to catch saltwater fish.

This is what happened when James invited a group of his friends to go fishing with him on a charter boat one Sunday afternoon in 1890. Unlike James, a skilled fisherman, most of his pals had never been on a fishing boat before that day. Everyone arrived on time and were soon fitted with rods, reels, tackle, and bait. His friends began to tease one another, making bets as to who would catch the first fish and reel in the largest tuna.

As the boat made its way to the fishing grounds, James tried to give his pals tips on catching fish. He was delighted with the bets they were making, knowing he would surely win them all.

The blues began to bite within minutes of arriving at the fishing banks. One after another, his pals hooked the hungry fish and reeled them in. Everyone was cheering and congratulating one another.

Meanwhile, James didn't get so much as a nibble on his line. His friends had all caught at least one or two fish, but he hadn't even gotten a bite. He grumbled to himself and shouted to them, "It's just beginner's luck! Just wait till I get started."

The more his pals laughed, the more annoyed James felt. Just as he began to regret inviting them on the trip, something big took his bait. With a giant upward jerk of his rod, he set the hook and began to fight what he knew was a prize-winning bluefish.

He could tell it was huge. It was heavier than anything he had ever hooked, and it was determined not to be caught. The giant fish yanked yards and yards of fishing line from his reel as it fought to loosen the hook.

His friends cheered as James battled the monster fish. Sweat was streaming down his face, his arms were throbbing, and he had stabbing pains in his back, but he could not give up.

Just as James brought the fish to the surface,

someone shouted, "Shark!" The captain raced to the deck with his shotgun and fired at the shark. A crewman speared the animal with a harpoon, and it was finally yanked over the rail onto the deck.

Everyone was still cheering when the shark smashed its tail down on the deck so hard that the entire boat shook. The crew ordered people away from the frenzied animal, which was bashing anything within reach.

While James and his friends stood to the side, the crew lassoed the shark's tail and tied it down. Finally, the shark stopped moving. James rushed to measure his catch. It was nearly six feet long. Everyone came closer to get a good look at its huge mouth full of razor-sharp teeth, and then it was rolled back into the sea.

No one was injured and the boat was not

damaged. James was very proud that he had caught a shark when his pals only got bluefish. He did say that if he ever gets another shark on his line, he will cut the line and not bring it on board.

These reports prove that bringing a shark onboard a boat isn't good for either the captain or crew, and is *especially* unpleasant for the shark.

ODD & CURIOUS SHARK ENCOUNTERS ALONG THE SHORE

There have been about sixty shark attacks along the Jersey Shore since 1842. A few of these are unlike any others, and they are both curious and somewhat amusing.

We usually think that shark attacks in New Jersey take place in the Atlantic Ocean. Would you believe that a shark once attacked a man one hundred and fifty miles from the Jersey Shore? It's true. In 2009, a scuba diver working at Adventure Aquarium in Camden, New Jersey, was bitten by a shark.

On that Sunday morning, two divers entered the shark tank to make minor repairs. As John, one of the divers, stepped off the safety ladder into the water, he bumped into something. Before he could turn to look, huge jaws grabbed ahold of his leg in a vice-like grip.

When he spun around, there was a seven-foot sand tiger shark with its jaws firmly attached to his leg. Then, just as suddenly as it had chomped down on his calf, the shark released its grip and swam away. John was treated for fifteen deep slashes on his leg. He recovered and soon returned to work. The sand tiger shark remained on display.

Although scientists tell us that sharks are fussy eaters and that humans really aren't on their menu, it can be disturbing to learn what has been found in the stomachs of sharks at the Jersey Shore. When a Lavallette fishing boat captured an eight-hundred-pound shark, they discovered it had eaten a twenty-pound turtle *and* a man's leg, which was still wearing its sock and shoe. The identity of the man who lost that leg is not known.

In nearby Spring Lake, vacationers on board a charter fishing boat were shocked when one of them managed to pull in a shark. It was very exciting for everyone, especially when they cut open the shark's stomach and found a woman's foot, still wearing a tan shoe. There were no missing women in the area, and the case remains unsolved.

Most people believe that humans can outsmart a shark. In one case, the sailors did not believe they could lose when they declared war on a group of sharks. It was a hot August afternoon in 1891, and two large wooden schooners, the *Mary C. Brown* and the *William Briggs*, were anchored side by side in the Longport, New Jersey harbor. The crews of the two ships were sitting on the deck enjoying a cool breeze when someone spotted a small group of sharks—also known as a shiver—prowling the water around the ships.

The men called back and forth between the two ships, each crew claiming to be better shark hunters than the other. As the sharks came closer, the men began to harpoon and shoot at them.

Several were wounded and three of the sharks were killed.

The teasing continued, and soon the sailors agreed to compete to see which crew could kill the most sharks. They were laughing and joking as they lowered their small rowboats into the water.

The men crammed into the little boats carrying harpoons, axes, clubs, and even a gun. Although the small boats were overcrowded, they didn't care. They had declared war on the sharks!

Everyone was still laughing and joking as they rowed away from their ships. They had not gone far when they sighted a huge shark fin. The men cheered. It was a giant shark, and they were out to get it! But it was not just one shark, it was *dozens* of angry sharks hovering together and heading toward them. Suddenly, the water seemed to turn a muddy gray as hundreds of sharks appeared.

Before the men could react, the sharks rushed them, swimming circles around their little boats. The sounds of splintering wood echoed across the water as the sharks rammed the boats with their huge snouts. While some men began shooting or stabbing at the beasts, others were busy bailing water from the bottom of their boats. They were nipped by sharp teeth and butted by enormous snouts. Sharks came from every direction, snapping their jagged teeth at the sailors.

It was all the men could do to stay afloat. The flashing teeth of the angry gray mob followed close behind as the men rowed away as fast as they could. In the end, the sharks chased them all the way back to the harbor.

There were no prizes waiting for the crews when they returned that day. The captains of their ships did not want to hear that they had killed three sharks. They only wanted the holes in the bottom of the boats repaired and the wounded men back on duty.

This time, the sharks won the war.

SHARKS: THE BIG FISH WITH THE BAD REPUTATION

Sharks get a bad rap! It doesn't matter if it is a movie, book, or TV show, sharks are always the bad guys. You'd think sharks do nothing but hover around our beaches just waiting for people to stick their feet into the water so they can charge in and bite off their toes. Sometimes sharks are described as killing machines or even "man-eaters." None of this is true.

Sharks truly are very fussy eaters, and people are not on their menu. (Perhaps sharks feel like you do when the school cafeteria serves mystery meat and cabbage for lunch.) Yes, sharks may bite to investigate whether or not a creature in their path could be prey—sometimes with deadly results. Unfortunately, even an exploratory bite can be dangerous or even fatal for a human. But sharks do not see people as prey, nor do they hunt humans as a source of food. Just as you would rather skip the mystery meat at school, a shark would much rather feed on fish and other marine animals.

Small sharks eat shrimp, krill, crabs, and small fish. Larger ones dine on larger fish, small dolphins, seals, turtles, and even seagulls. Perhaps we are not on the shark's menu because we taste like the cheeseburgers and French fries we eat. That is something in our favor!

In most cases, when a shark bites someone, it is a case of mistaken identity. They see arms and legs thrashing about in the water, and they simply mistake it for prey.

Although they have a bad reputation, scientists know sharks are important to the ocean's food chain. As some of the largest fish predators in the ocean, they help keep the food chain balanced so it is possible for all sorts of sea creatures to exist in the world's oceans.

Although sharks are found in nearly all the world's oceans, they are not eating everything in sight. Some species prefer to live in very cold waters, while others spend their entire lives in warm tropical regions. Some sharks never travel far from their birthplace, while others migrate, swimming thousands of miles each year from one location to another.

Around five hundred species of sharks can be found in the world's oceans. Along the Jersey Shore, there are only a few dozen different kinds of sharks, most of which are harmless to humans. You are unlikely to spot more than a handful of different kinds of sharks along the shore. Some local sharks hang out in shallow waters along the shore, while others spend their time in the deeper waters offshore and never come near the coast.

Sharks do not live up to their bad reputation, but one could still ruin a day at the beach for you and your friends. Be sure to check out "Before You Go" on the next page to learn some lifeguard-suggested tips for staying safe while enjoying the beautiful Jersey Shore.

BEFORE YOU GO: LIFEGUARD-APPROVED SAFETY TIPS

Although we know most sharks in Jersey Shore waters are harmless, we also know shark attacks can happen. When they do, it can quickly become a life-and-death situation. Here are some simple lifeguard-approved safety tips for all beachgoers.

1. Never swim alone.

2. Never swim anywhere without lifeguards.

3. Always follow lifeguards' directions. They aren't playing around when they tell you to get out of the water. That means there is danger.

4. If you see a fin sticking out of the water, get on shore and tell the lifeguard.

5. Avoid swimming at dawn or dusk, when sharks like to feed.

6. Don't swim where there are schools (large groups) of small baitfish. Often, they are being chased by larger fish such as sharks.

7. If you see a large or unusual fish in the water, get back to shore immediately. Better safe than sorry.

8. Don't wear shiny jewelry or play with shiny objects in the surf—it may attract sharks.

9. Never tease or injure an animal of any kind.

10. If you see a sick or injured fish or shark, do not touch it. Report this to an adult.

Patricia Heyer is a local history buff with a special interest in New Jersey folklore and marine science. She has written extensively for both children and adults during her career. Her most recent title, *The Ghostly Tales of the Jersey Shore* was released in 2023. Pat is an avid reader, beachcomber, and animal rescue supporter. She resides on the Jersey Shore with her husband, Rob, and their rescue cat, Gracie. Visit www.heyerwriter.com to learn more!

Dive into even more books by Patricia Heyer!

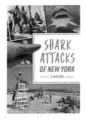